The Illuminated Calendar For 1845: Copied From The Hours Of Anne Of Brittany...

Anonymous

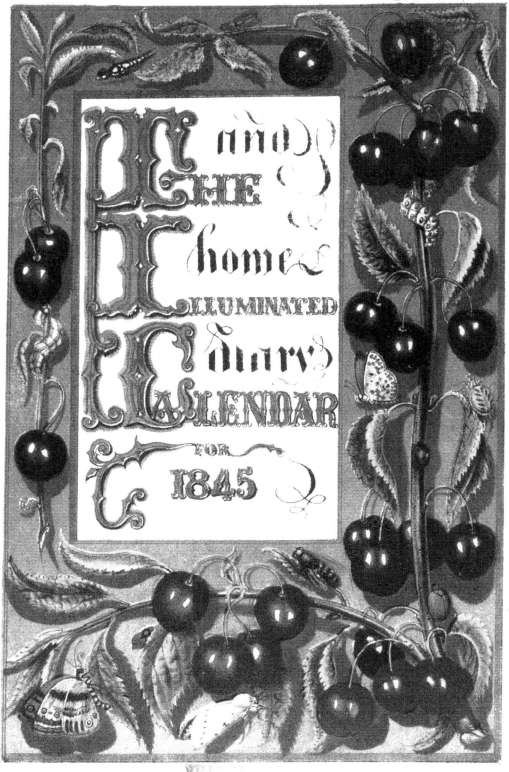

John
THE
home
ILLUMINATED
Diary
CALENDAR
FOR
1845

Description of the Illuminated Calendar,
Copied from the Hours of Anne of Brittany.

" The Hours of Anne of Brittany" is a magnificent prayer book preserved in the Bibliotheque Royale of Paris. This splendid work, of handsome quarto size, commences with a beautiful Calendar, executed in body colour in the finest style of miniature painting of the period. Each subject occupies an entire page, with the exception of the tablet in the centre of the picture, which contains a portion of the Saints' days of the Roman Calendar, the other portion on the opposite page being ornamented only with a border, representing a flower, evidently painted from nature, on a gold ground. Hence it will be seen that, with the exception of the adaptation of the Almanack to 1845, the present work is exactly copied from the original. The remainder of the manuscript volume contains prayers to all the principal saints, with a finely executed miniature, occupying an entire page, taken from the legend of each particular saint. Some of the prayers opposite to these pictures are ornamented with borders similar to those of the Calendar, whilst others are entirely framed in borders of richer character, of which that on our title page is a good, though not one of the most elaborate specimens. Other prayers and offices are similarly enriched, and in all there are upwards of three hundred plants portrayed, the whole of them executed with great beauty, and with sufficient fidelity, to render the volume the most complete herbal of the period. The subjects which form the illustration of each month are exceedingly happy. Thus, for the bleak month of January we find a snow storm, with a traveller seeking shelter in a building, where, from the preparations seen going on, his reception will evidently be hospitable: the upper part of the picture, as in all the others, is occupied by the sign of the zodiac, which is well detached by its purely decorative treatment. In February we have the in-door comforts of home and shelter illustrated, which by a bold section,—a common device of illuminators, —is made to contrast strikingly with the frigid and snow-covered exterior. March exhibits the earliest field occupation—A man is engaged pruning the trees of an orchard, while a young woman collects the croppings for firewood; and in the back ground, knights in armour are seen issuing from the gates of a castle. These elaborately drawn castles are not the least interesting portion of the volume. We still admire the crumbling ruins on the vine clad hills of the Rhine, and the more undulating banks of the Loire or Garonne; but here we see them exhibited in all their original perfection, sketched by a contemporary artist. In April, spring has already her enamelled carpet of flowers, and the fair chatelaine is enjoying her lofty flower garden on the castle terrace, accompanied by female attendants, who present her with chaplets. The month of May is treated with peculiar elegance, the zodiacal sign of the Twins being beautifully reproduced in the picture by twin brothers returning from gathering the May or hawthorn flowers. June exhibits the hay-cutting, and the two mowers are so naturally treated, that one may almost hear the rural sound of scythe whetting, and feel the dewy freshness of a bright June morning. July represents the harvest. August brings the winnowing of the grain; September the vintage. October exhibits the sower, and the landscape portion of this subject is among the most successful; the mill-pool with its sedgy banks, and the swans, doubled by their reflections on its glassy surface, are beautiful realities which the illuminator has fully appreciated, and has treated with an excellence seldom attained even by the great masters of the period. In November, the swine-herd conducts his drove to the oak wood, where they are feasting and fattening upon the falling crop of acorns. December represents a scene in the preparations for the good cheer of Christmas—one pig is already prepared, and another is held down by the nervous arm of a resolute housewife to receive the knife, while a girl stirs the blood destined for the black puddings, one of the favourite delicacies of our forefathers.

The work was probably executed about the year 1499, on the occasion of the marriage of Anne with her second husband, Louis the Twelfth.

Anne of Brittany, only daughter and heiress of Francis the Second, Duke of Brittany, was born in the year 1476, and losing her father at the age of fourteen, became, with such a dowry as the duchy of Brittany, an object of contention among many powerful suitors. Eventually she gave her hand to Maximilian, the King of the Romans, to whom she had been affianced by her father, and the marriage was secretly performed, by proxy, with the customary ridiculous ceremony. Meanwhile the celebrated Count Dunois, frustrated in his endeavour to obtain her hand for his patron and friend the Duke of Orleans, then a state prisoner, resolved at all hazards to annex the duchy of Brittany to the crown of France; and having gained the consent of his master, Charles the Eighth, to open negotiations for her marriage with that Prince, he, by dint of threats and artifices, at last gained his point, and Anne of Brittany became Queen of France in 1491. On the death of Charles, in 1498, she was at first overwhelmed with grief; but rousing herself from her despondency, she hastened to Brittany, where she resumed the exercise of her hereditary sovereignty, and in less than four months the young and charming widow gave her hand to Louis the Twelfth, who, when Duke of Orleans, had been one of her suitors; thus becoming a second time Queen of France.

Her court, which was remarkable for its splendour, was frequented by many young ladies of quality, both French and Breton, whose education and deportment she directed by precept and example; and it is a remarkable fact, that these ladies were the first termed "Maids of honour." She is said to have been the first Queen to adopt black as mourning on the death of her first husband; white having been the royal mourning previously to her time.

The present is an attempt to render mechanism an auxiliary of art, as far as it is now practicable, and to point the way to greater and higher efforts. The flower borders are printed entirely by the lithographic press of Mr. Owen Jones, and it is believed are excellent specimens of that delicate process. The figure subjects are coloured by hand.

This volume will answer every purpose of the usual Almanacks, and "The Diary" will furnish the means of recording interesting occurrences and home events, which being registered in a volume of intrinsic worth, will thus form a more permanent record than the usual pages of Diaries and Almanacks.

*** It is intended to publish annually a volume of similar character.

January

Diary

Ilex agrifolium

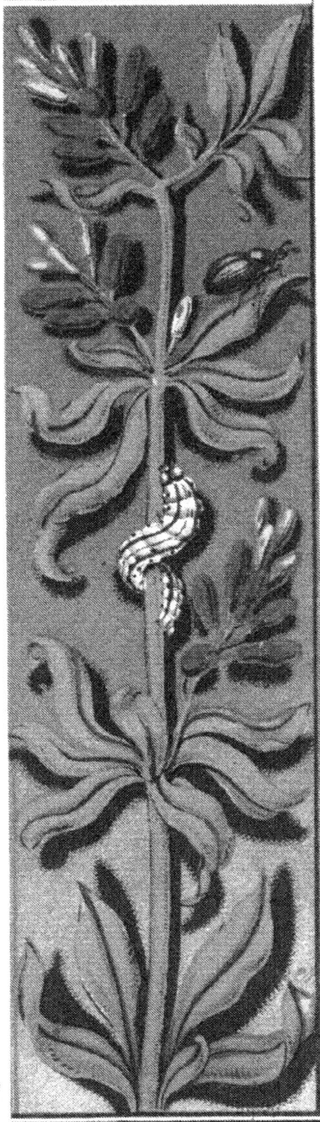

Vingnetier

1	
2	
3	
4	
5	
6	
7	
8	
9	
10	
11	
12	
13	
14	
15	
16	

January

diary

Cosolida minor

Margarites

17	
18	
19	
20	
21	
22	
23	
24	
25	
26	
27	
28	
29	
30	
31	

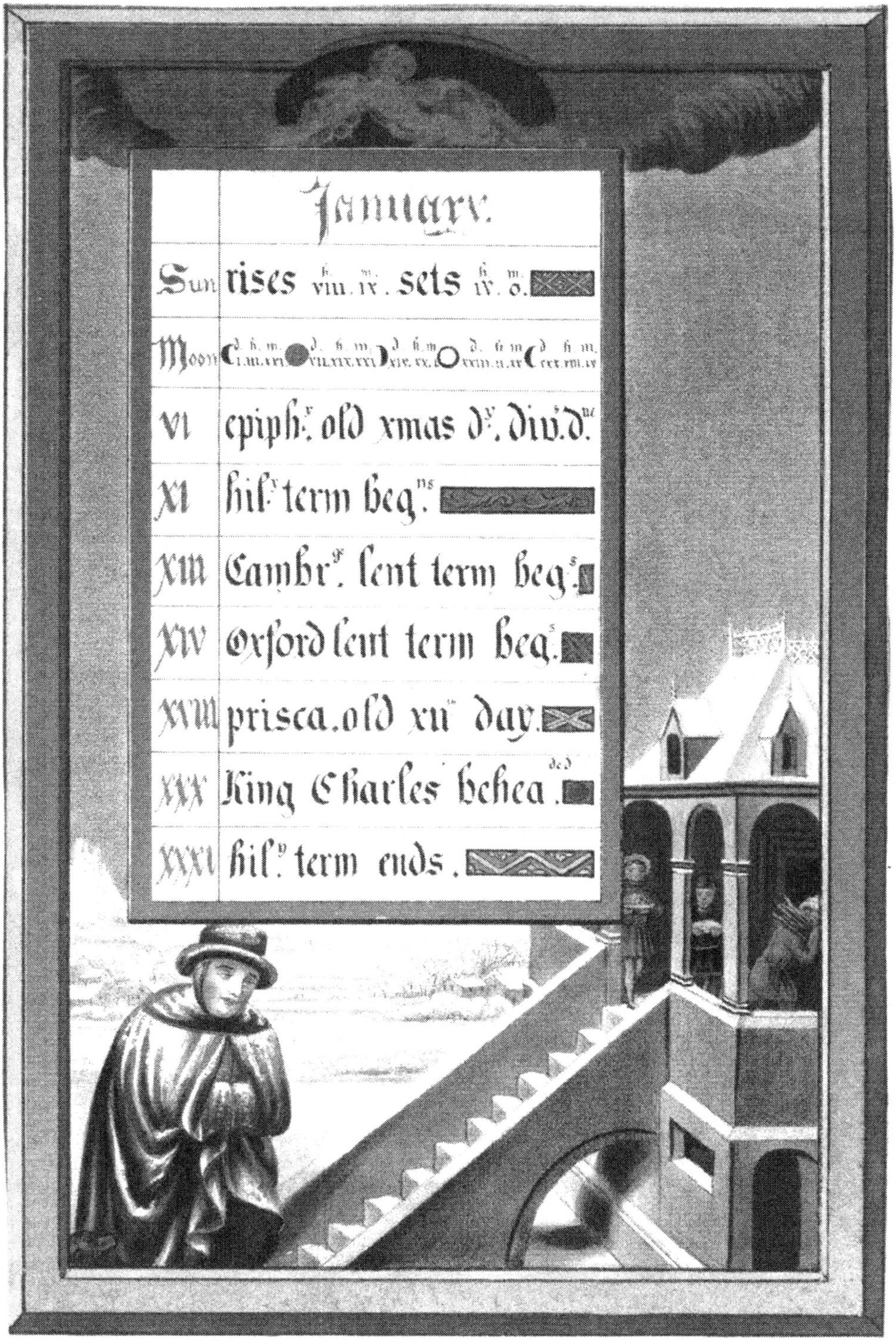
January.
Sun rises h. m. viii. ix. sets h. m. iv. o.
Moon
vi epiph.y old xmas dy. div.d.nd
xi hil.y term beg.ns
xiii Cambr.g lent term beg.s
xiv Oxford lent term beg.s
xviii prisca. old xii.th day.
xxx King Charles behea.ded
xxxi hil.y term ends.

February.

Diary.

Menuta Pẽsela

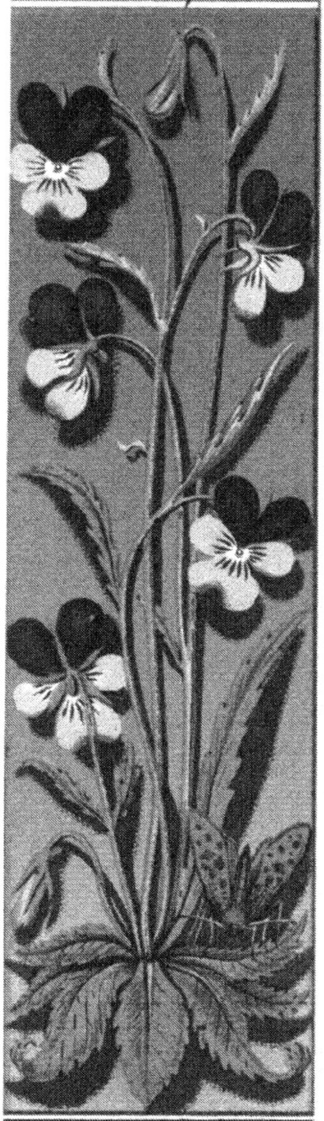

Pansees

1	
2	
3	
4	
5	
6	
7	
8	
9	
10	
11	
12	
13	
14	
15	
16	

February diary

Cephagrossium

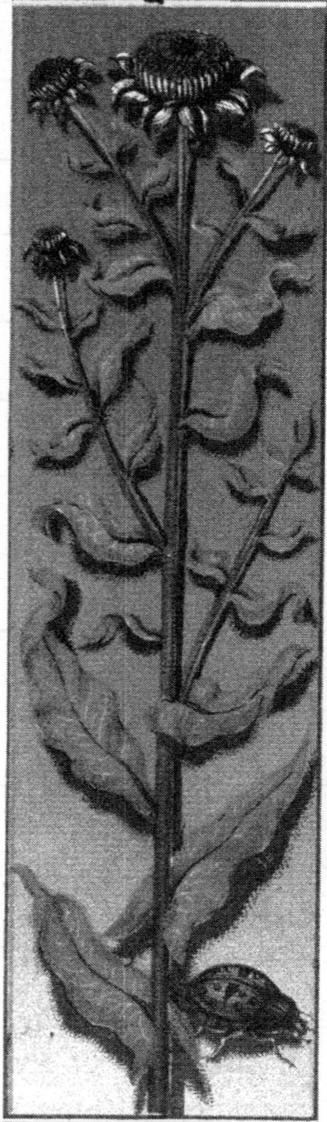

Grousse testes

M	17	
T	18	
W	19	
T	20	
F	21	
S	22	
S	23	
M	24	
T	25	
W	26	
T	27	
F	28	

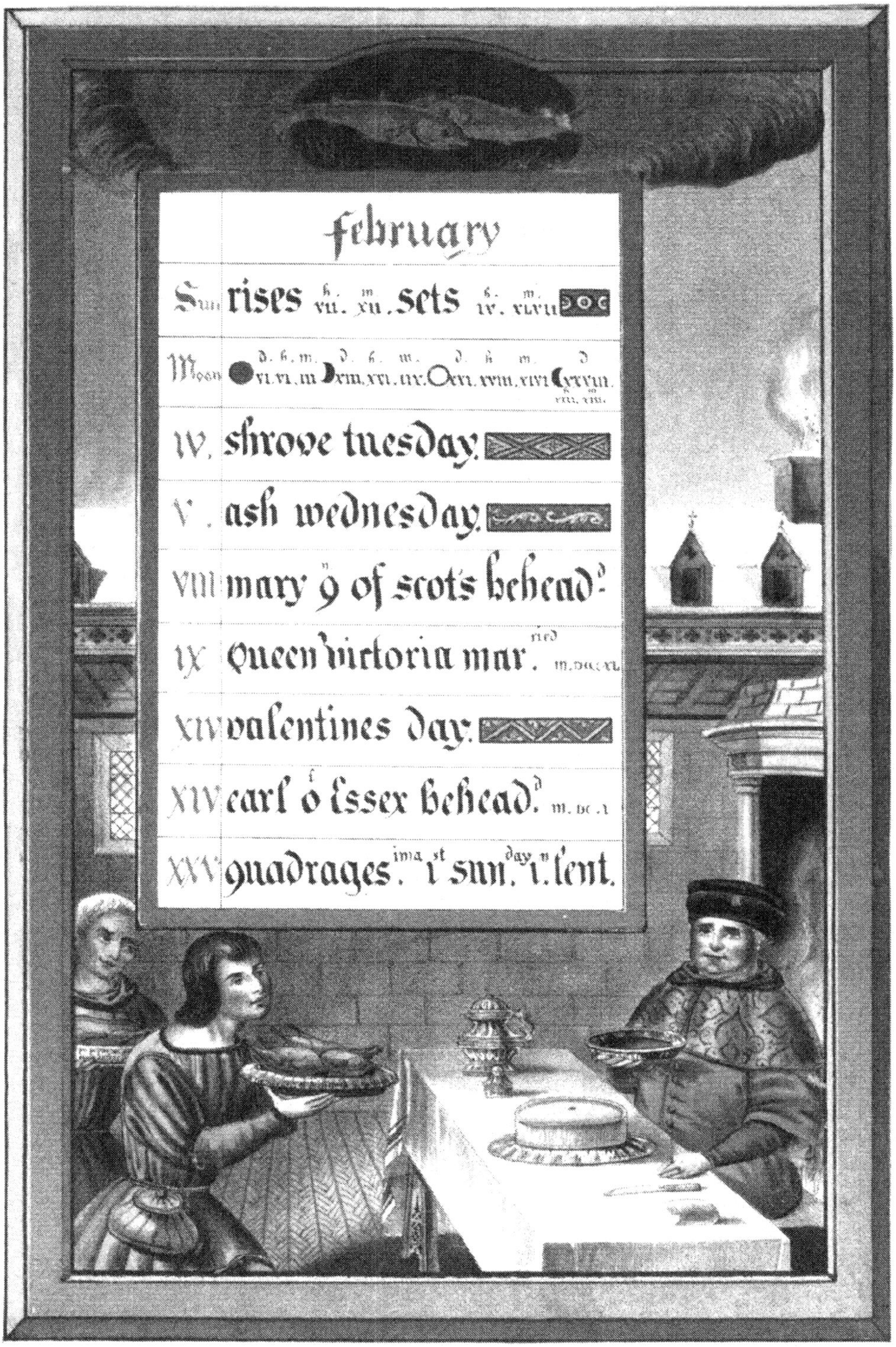
February
Sun rises h. vii. m. xii. sets h. iv. m. xlvii.
Moon d. h. m. vi. vi. iii. d. h. m. xiii. xvi. lix. d. h. m. xxi. xviii. xlvi. d. xxviii. h. xxx. m. xiii.
iv. shrove tuesday.
v. ash wednesday.
viii mary q of scot's behead.d
ix Queen victoria mar.ried m.dcccxl.
xiv valentines day.
xxv earl o' Essex behead.d m.dci
xxv quadrages.ima 1st sun.day n' 1. lent.

VILLE DE LYON

Biblioth. du Palais des Arts

march
Diary

Viola

Violete de marc

1
2
3
4
5
6
7
8
9
10
11
12
13
14
15
16

march
diary.

Specie cardo

Garoffle

17	
18	
19	
20	
21	
22	
23	
24	
25	
26	
27	
28	
29	
30	
31	

March

Sun rises vi. vim. sets v. xxxviii.

Moon ● ... vii. xviii. xxxvi. Der. ou. iii. ○ xviii. vii. ii. (xxx. v. o.

1 S: David's day.

XIV Cambrid⁵ᵉ lent term ends.

XV Oxford lent term ends.

XVI palm sunday.

XVII S¹ Patrick.

XXI good friday.

XXIII easter sunday.

april
diary.

Buglossa

Bugleuse

1	
2	
3	
4	
5	
6	
7	
8	
9	
10	
11	
12	
13	
14	
15	
16	

april
diary

Blad. turgine

17

18

19

20

21

22

23

24

25

26

27

28

29

30

Ble de turgnie

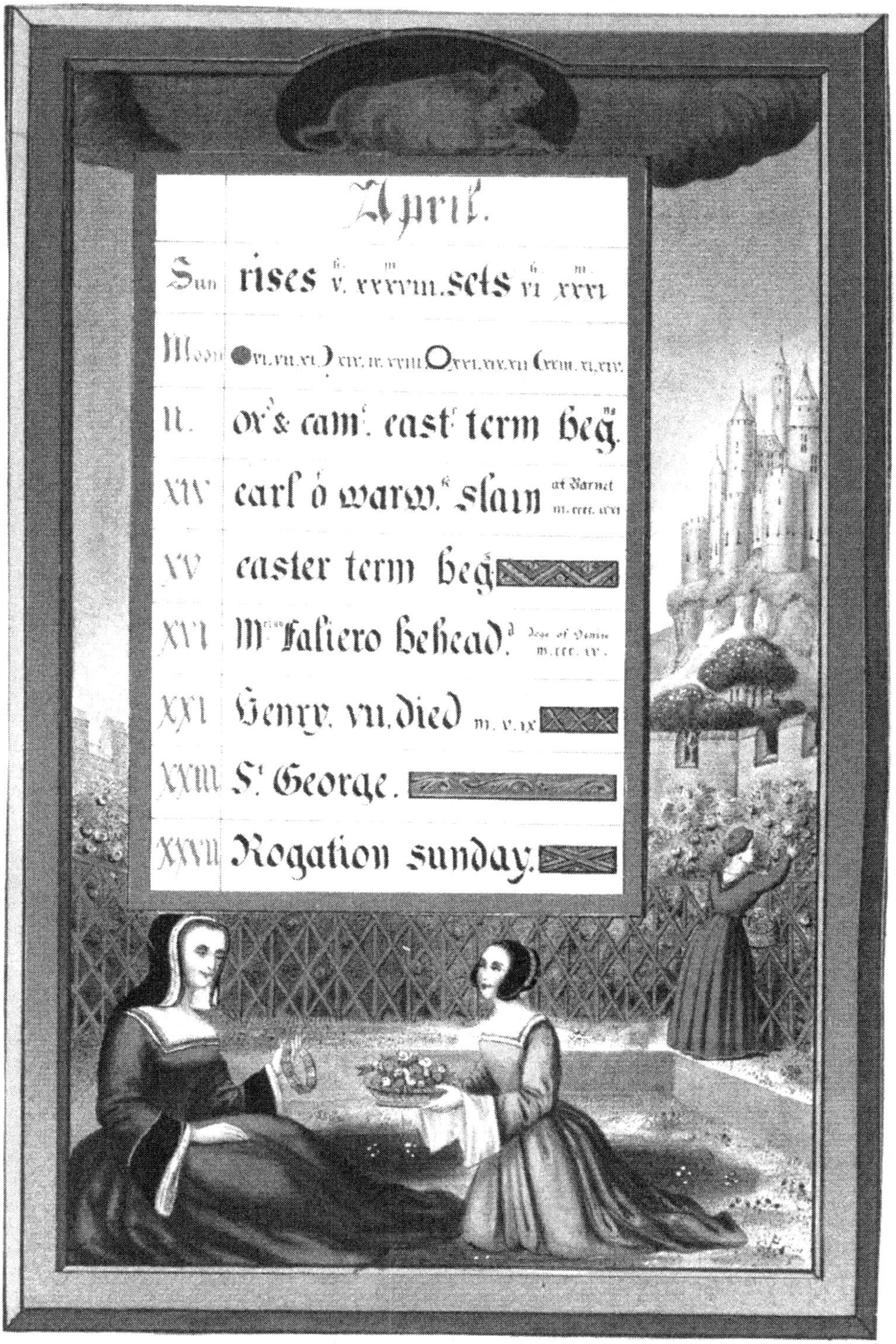
April.
Sun rises h. v. m. xxxviii. sets h. vi m. xxvi
Moon vi.vii.xi. xiv.ix.xviii. xxi.xix.xii xxix.xi.xiv.
ii. ox.d & cam.e east.r term beg.ns
xiv earl o.f warw.k slain at Barnet m.cccc.lxxi
xv easter term beg.s
xvi M.arino Faliero behead.d Doge of Venice m.ccc.lv.
xxi Henry. vii. died m. v. ix
xxiii S.t George.
xxvii Rogation sunday.

may

diary

Gimbaleria

Damoyselles

1	
2	
3	
4	
5	
6	
7	
8	
9	
10	
11	
12	
13	
14	
15	
16	

MAY.
diary.

Centaurea maior

Menuly

17	
18	
19	
20	
21	
22	
23	
24	
25	
26	
27	
28	
29	
30	
31	

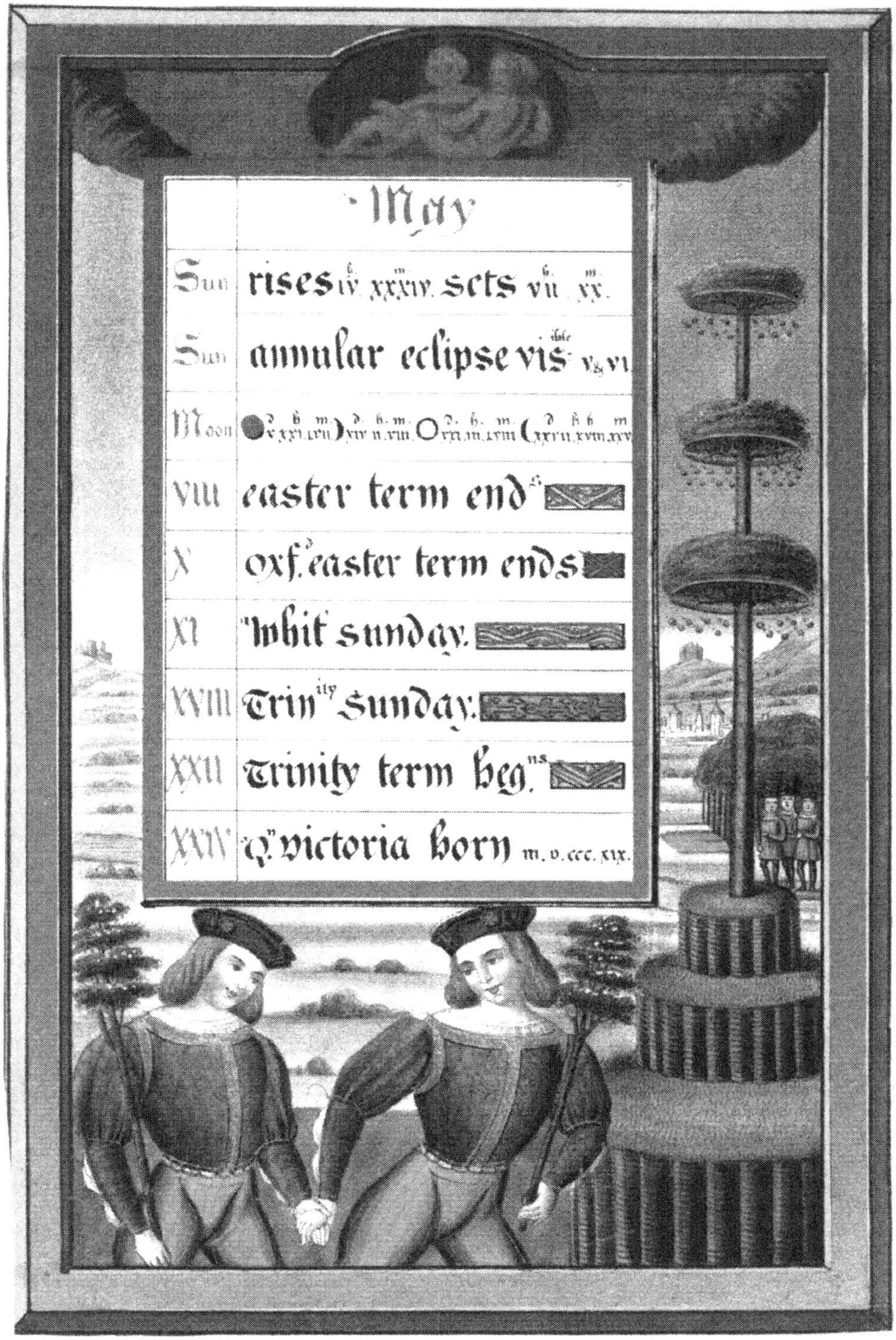
May
Sun rises iv. xxxiv. sets vii. xx.
Sun annular eclipse visible v & vi
Moon
viii easter term ends
x oxfd easter term ends
xi whit sunday.
xviii Trinity sunday.
xxii Trinity term begins
xxiv Qn victoria born m. d. ccc. xix.

June
diary

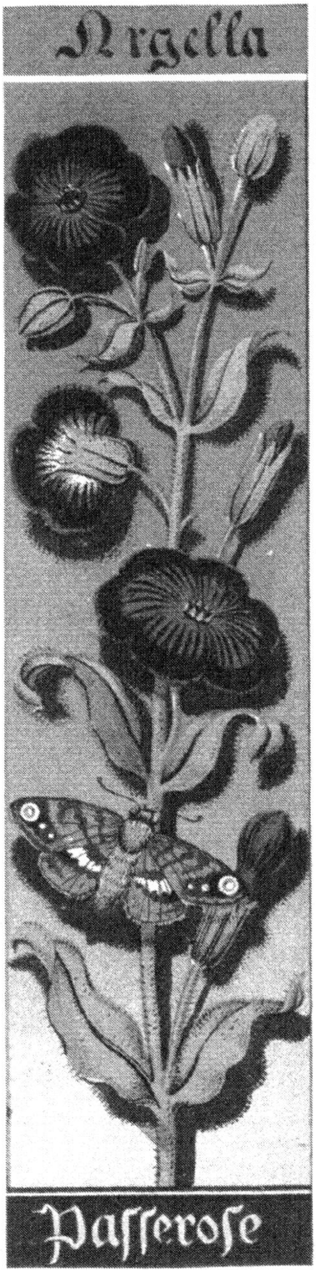
Nigella
Passerose

S	1	
M	2	
T	3	
W	4	
T	5	
F	6	
S	7	
S	8	
M	9	
T	10	
W	11	
T	12	
F	13	
S	14	
S	15	
M	16	

June.
diary.

Camamilla

Camamille

17	
18	
19	
20	
21	
22	
23	
24	
25	
26	
27	
28	
29	
30	

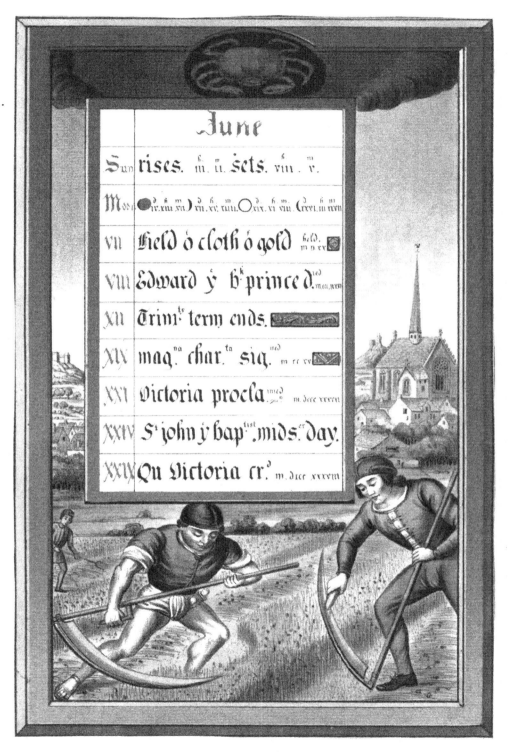

	June		
S	rises. m. ii. sets. viii. v.		
M			
VII	field o̊ cloth o̊ gold		
VIII	Edward ȳ b'ᵏ prince d.		
XII	Trim'ᵗʸ term ends.		
XIV	mag'ⁿᵃ char'ᵗᵃ sig.		
XXI	Victoria procla		
XXIV	St john ȳ bap'ᵗˢᵗ mids'ʳ day.		
XXVI	Qu Victoria cr'ᵈ		

July
diary.

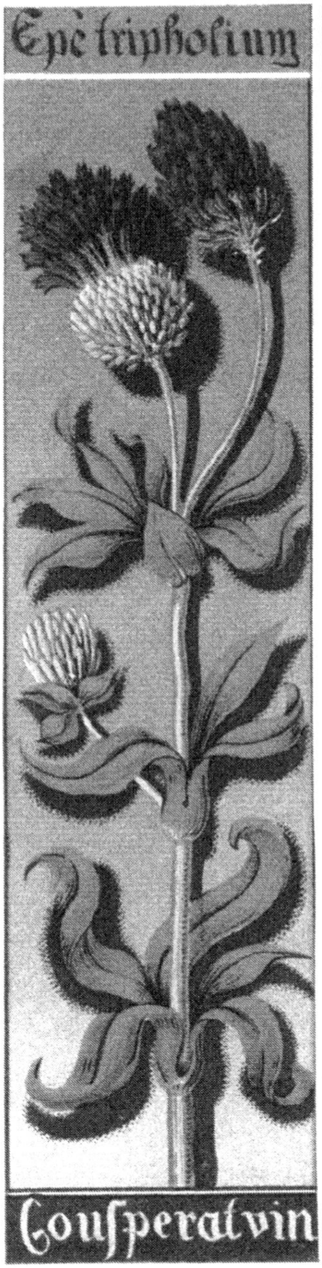

Epè triphosium
Cousperatvin

T 1	
M 2	
T 3	
F 4	
S 5	
S 6	
M 7	
T 8	
W 9	
T 10	
F 11	
S 12	
S 13	
M 14	
T 15	
W 16	

July Diary

Linum

Du lin

T	17	
F	18	
S	19	
S	20	
M	21	
T	22	
W	23	
T	24	
F	25	
S	26	
S	27	
M	28	
T	29	
W	30	
T	31	

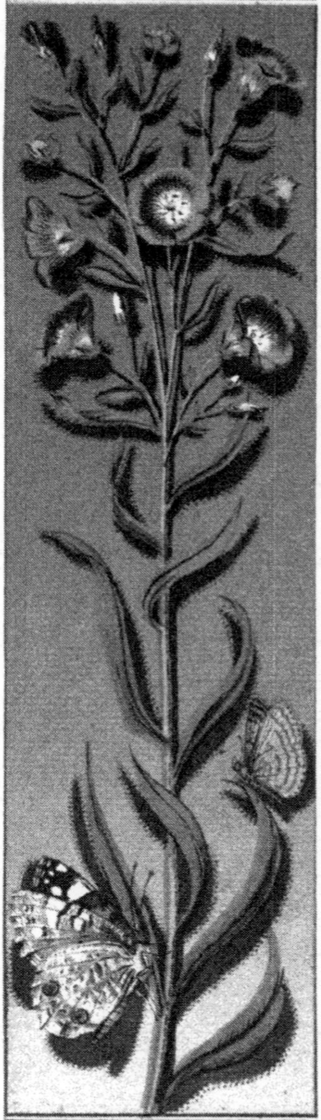

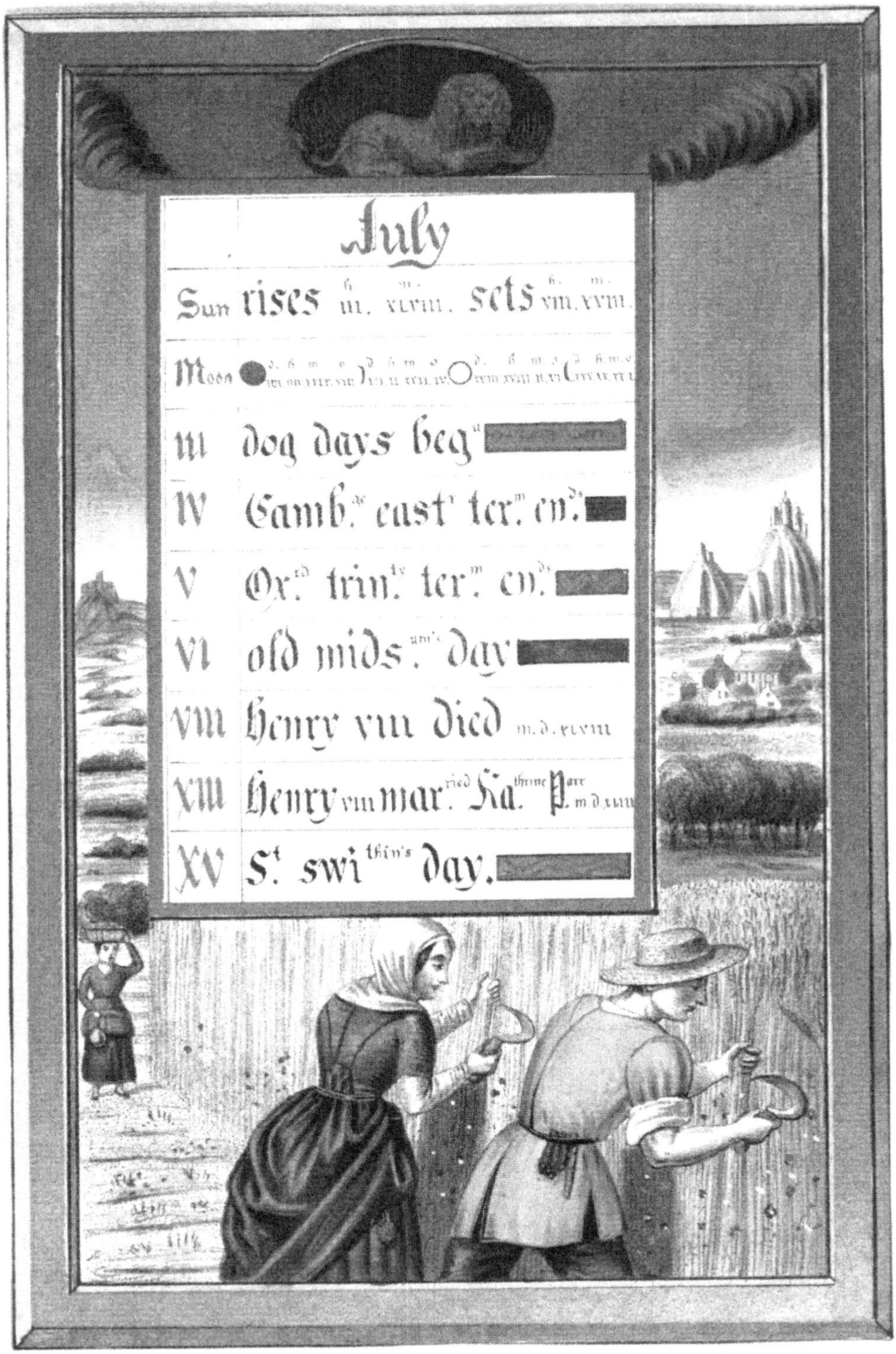
July
Sun rises iii. xlviii. sets viii. xviii.
Moon
iii dog days beg^n
iv Camb.^ge east^r ter.^m en.^ds
v Ox.^rd trin.^ty ter.^m en.^ds
vi old mids.^um^r day
viii Henry viii died m.d.xlvii
xii Henry viii mar.^ried Ka.^therine P.^arr m.d.xliii
xv S^t. swi^thin's day.

August

diary

Iris

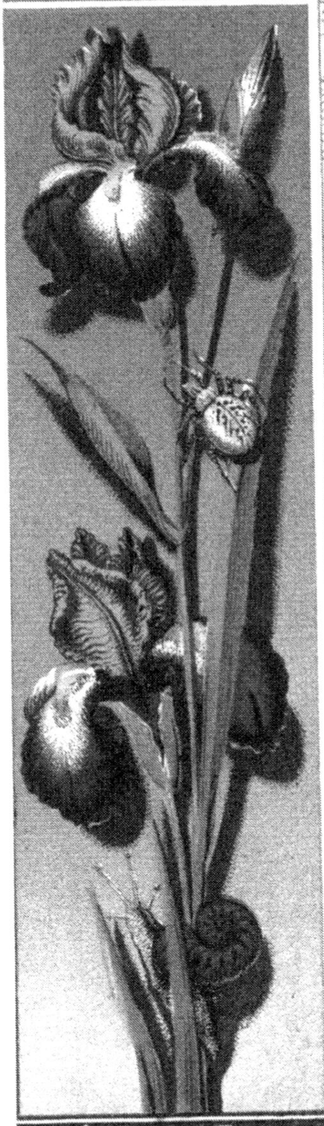

Flambe

F	1	
S	2	
S	3	
M	4	
T	5	
W	6	
T	7	
F	8	
S	9	
S	10	
M	11	
T	12	
W	13	
T	14	
F	15	
S	16	

august
diary.

Muleta

Meuidre

17
18
19
20
21
22
23
24
25
26
27
28
29
30
31

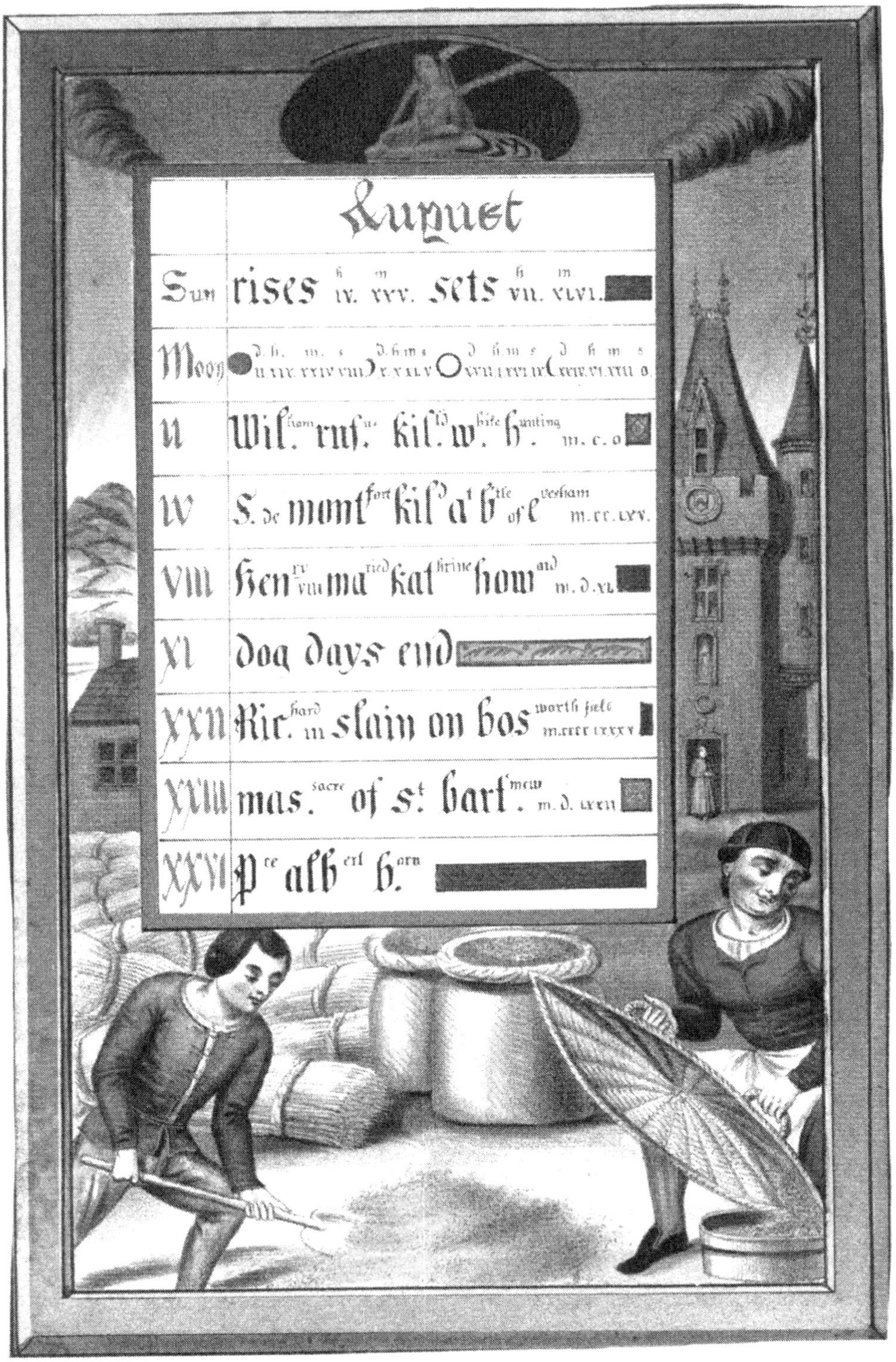
August
Sun rises h m iv. xxv. sets h m vii. xlvi.
Moon
ii Wil. ruf. kil. w. h. m. c. o
iv S. de mont.fort kil. a.t b.tle of e.vesham m. cc. lxv.
viii Hen.ry viii ma.ried kat.hrine how.ard m. d. xl.
xi dog days end
xxii Ric.hard iii slain on bos.worth field m. cccc. lxxxv
xxiii mas.sacre of st. bart.mew m. d. lxxii
xxvi P.ce alb.ert b.orn

september
diary

Undina

Andine

1	
2	
3	
4	
5	
6	
7	
8	
9	
10	
11	
12	
13	
14	
15	
16	

September

Diary

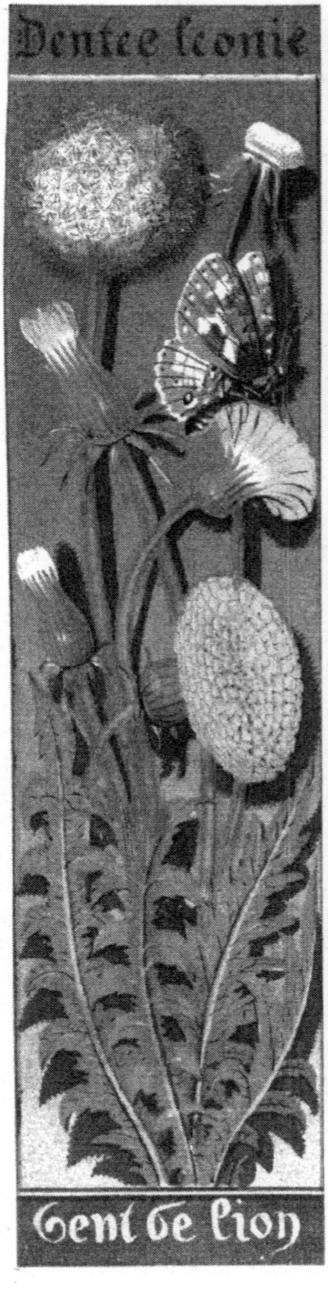

Dentes leonis
Dent de Lion

W	17	
T	18	
F	19	
S	20	
S	21	
M	22	
T	23	
W	24	
T	25	
F	26	
S	27	
S	28	
M	29	
T	30	

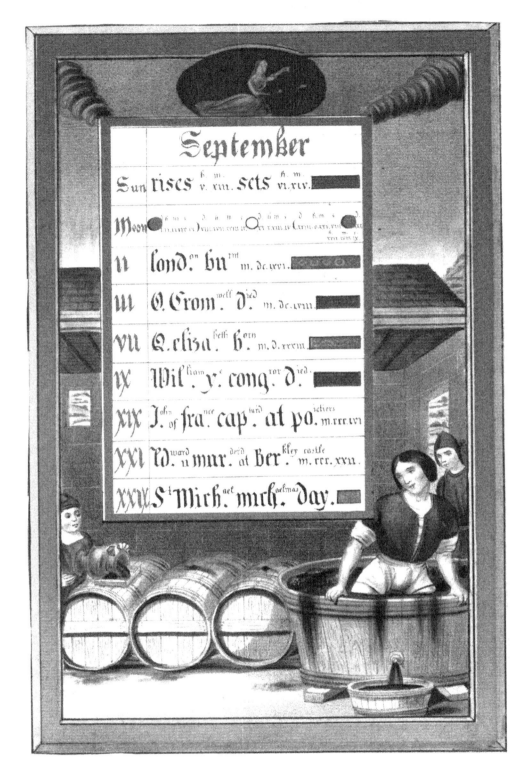

September

Sun	rises	h. m. v. viii.	sets	h. m. vi. xiv.

Moon

ii	lond.on bu.rnt	m. dc.xvi.
iii	O. Crom.well D.ied	m. dc.lviii.
vii	Q. eliza.beth b.orn	m. d. xxxiii.
ix	Wil.liam y.e conq.ror d.ied
xix	J.ohn of fra.nce cap.turd at po.ictiers m. ccc. lvi.
xxi	Ed.ward ii mur.derd at Ber.kley castle m. ccc. xxii.
xxix	St Mich.ael mich.aelmas day

October
Diary

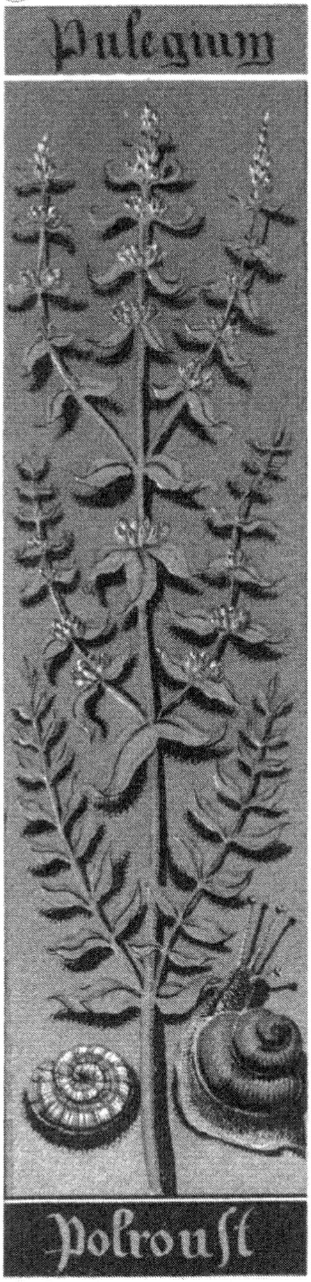
Pulegium
Polroust

1	
2	
3	
4	
5	
6	
7	
8	
9	
10	
11	
12	
13	
14	
15	
16	

october

diary

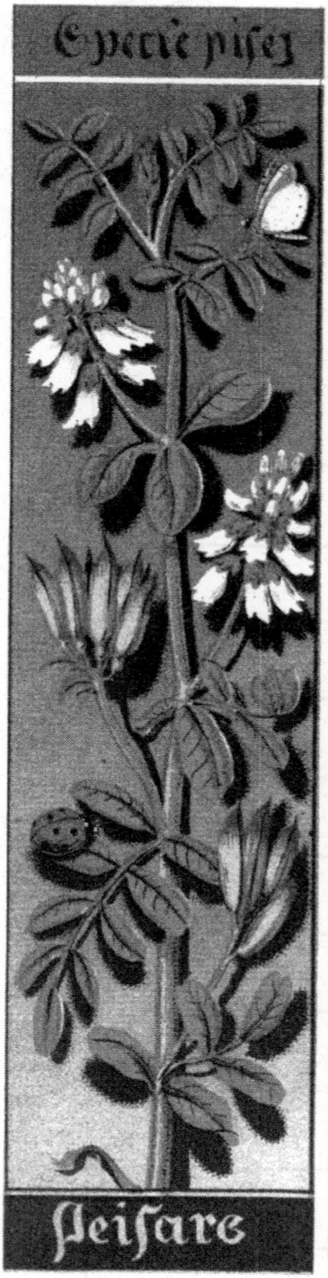

Peisare

F 17	
S 18	
S 19	
M 20	
T 21	
W 22	
T 23	
F 24	
S 25	
S 26	
M 27	
T 28	
W 29	
T 30	
F 31	

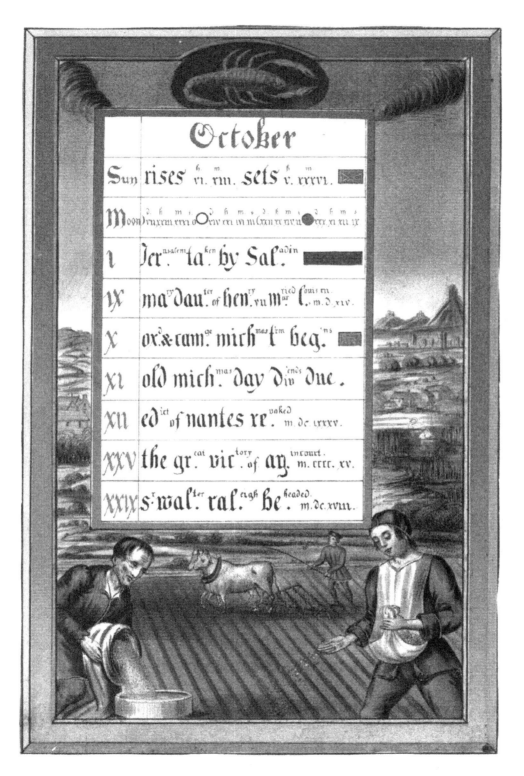

October

Sun rises ᴴ ᴹ vi. xiii. **sets** ᴴ ᴹ v. xxxvi.	
Moon rises ᴰ ᴴ ᴹ vi. xxiii. xxii o rises ᴰ ᴴ ᴹ xiv. xii. iii m sets ᴰ ᴴ ᴹ xxii. xiv. ii ● sets ᴰ ᴴ ᴹ xi. xii. ix	
I Jerᵘˢᵃˡᵉᵐ taᵏᵉⁿ by Salᵃᵈⁱⁿ	
IX maʳy dauᵗᵉʳ of henʳʸ vu maʳ ried Louis xⁱ. m. d. xiv.	
X oxᵈ & camᵇᵍᵉ michᵐᵃˢ tᵉʳᵐ begⁱⁿˢ	
XI old michᵐᵃˢ day divⁱᵉⁿᵈˢ Due.	
XII edⁱᶜᵗ of nantes reᵛᵒᵏᵉᵈ. m. dc. lxxxv.	
XXV the grᵉᵃᵗ vicᵗᵒʳʸ of ayⁱⁿ ᶜᵒᵘʳᵗ. m. cccc. xv.	
XXIX sᵗ walᵗᵉʳ ralᵉⁱᵍʰ beʰᵉᵃᵈᵉᵈ. m. dc. xviii.	

November

Diary.

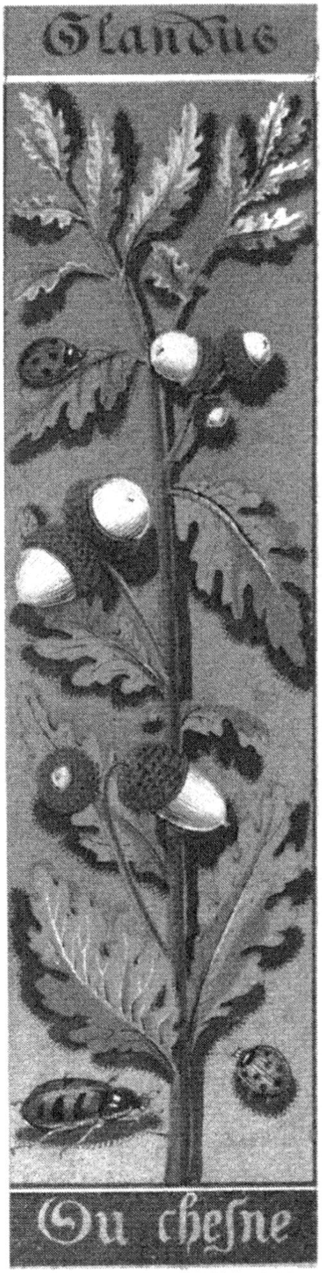
Glandus
Ou chesne

1	
2	
3	
4	
5	
6	
7	
8	
9	
10	
11	
12	
13	
14	
15	
16	

november
Diary.

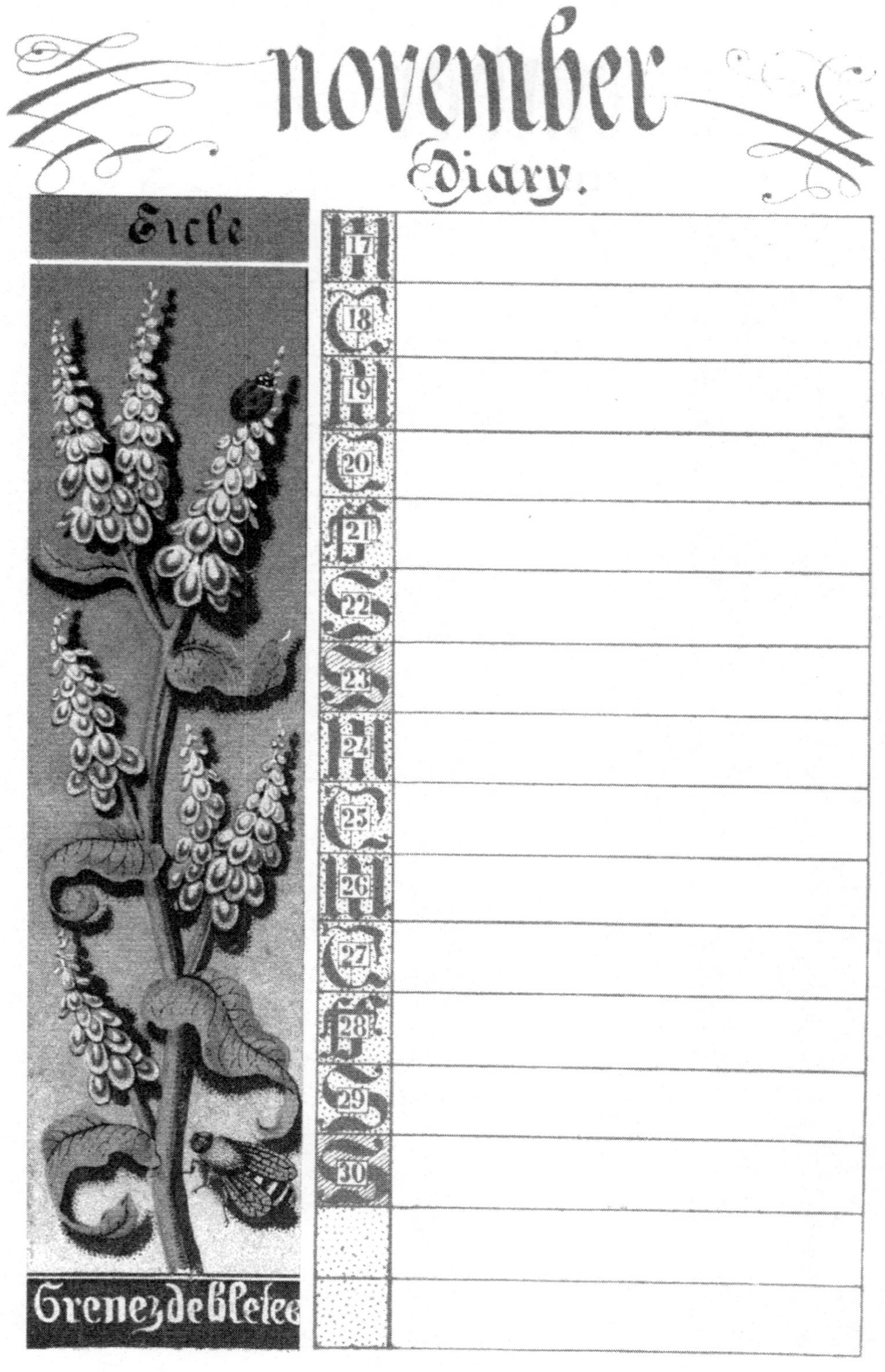
Ercle
Grenez de bletee

M 17	
T 18	
W 19	
T 20	
F 21	
S 22	
S 23	
M 24	
T 25	
W 26	
T 27	
F 28	
S 29	
S 30	

Nouember

Sun	rises vi. iv. sets iv. xxvii.		
Moon			
Moon	a partial eclipse		
ii	mich.mas ter.m beg.ns		
v	gun.powder plot		
ix	Lo.rd ma.yors day		
xxv	mich.as te.rm en.ds		
xxix	card.inal wolsey. di.ed		
xxx	St. And.rew		

December
diary.

Clanelarie

Berg de grue

1	
2	
3	
4	
5	
6	
7	
8	
9	
10	
11	
12	
13	
14	
15	
16	

december
diary.

rise agrisolium

Cu housl

17	
18	
19	
20	
21	
22	
23	
24	
25	
26	
27	
28	
29	
30	
31	

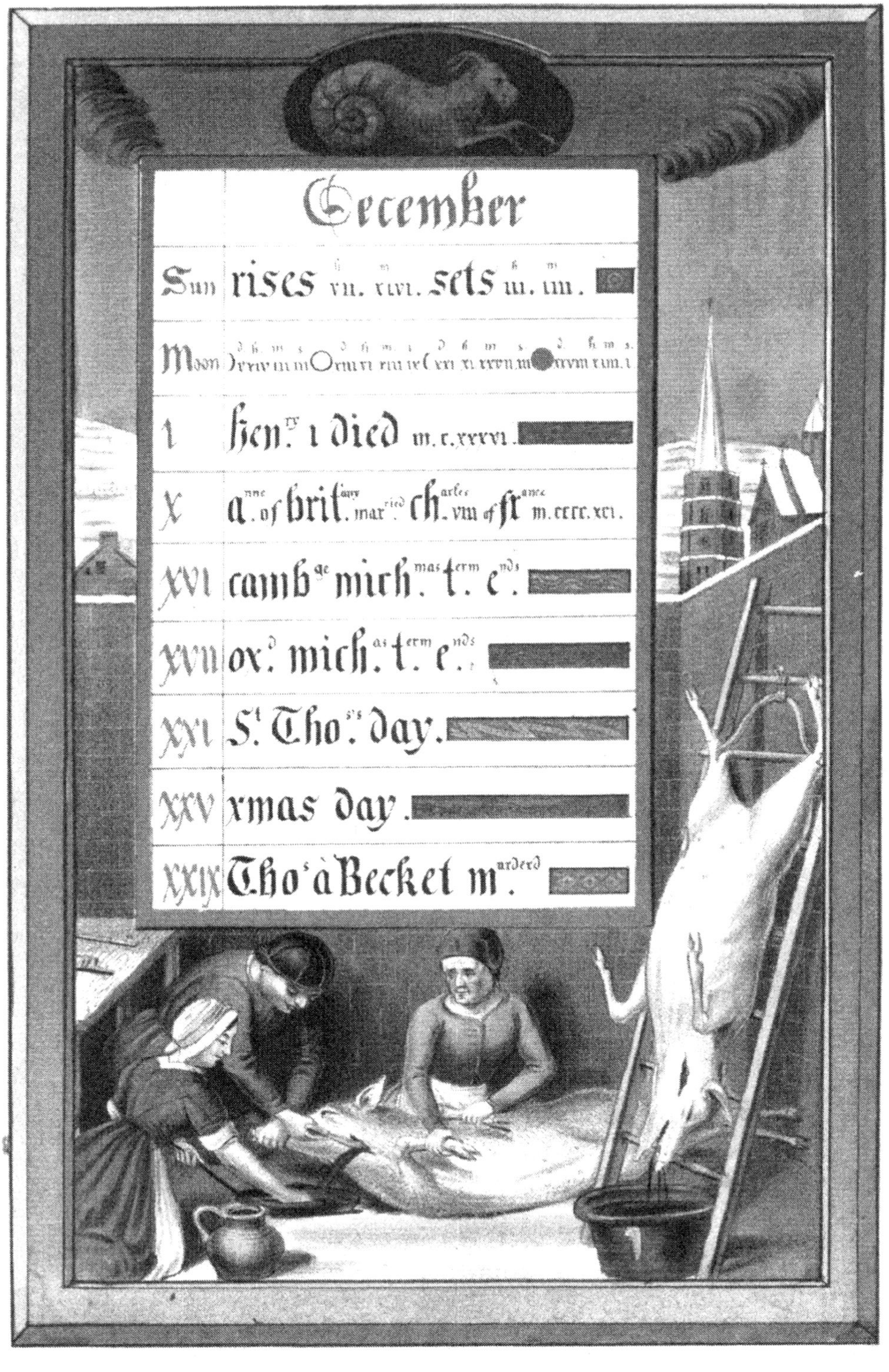
December
Sun rises vii. xlvi. sets iii. iiii.
i Henry i died m.c.xxxvi.
x Anne of brittany married Charles viii of France m.cccc.xci.
xvi cambge michmas term ends.
xvii oxd michas term ends
xxi St. Thos's day.
xxv xmas day.
xxix Thos à Becket murderd

Illuminated Books

PUBLISHED BY

MESSRS. LONGMAN, BROWN, GREEN, AND LONGMANS.

I.

A HISTORY OF ILLUMINATED BOOKS,

FROM THE IVth TO THE XVIIth CENTURY,

BY

HENRY NOEL HUMPHREYS:

ILLUSTRATED BY

A SERIES OF MAGNIFICENT SPECIMENS,

Consisting of an Entire Page of the Exact Size of the Original,

FROM THE MOST

Celebrated and Splendid MSS.

IN THE IMPERIAL AND ROYAL LIBRARIES OF VIENNA, MOSCOW, PARIS, NAPLES, COPENHAGEN, AND MADRID;—
FROM THE VATICAN, ESCURIAL, AMBROSIAN, AND OTHER GREAT LIBRARIES OF THE CONTINENT,
AND FROM THE RICH PUBLIC, COLLEGIATE, AND PRIVATE LIBRARIES OF GREAT BRITAIN;

SUPERBLY PRINTED IN GOLD, SILVER, AND COLOURS.

THOSE who have not visited the great libraries of Europe, and passed much time in searching for and examining the treasures of art contained in their vast and almost unknown stores of Illuminated MSS., cannot form the slightest idea of the extreme beauty of many of those wonderful productions of middle-age art—of their gorgeous colouring and gilding, their intricate and elaborate design—their endless variety—their delightful combinations of form and colour—and the extreme perfection of execution and extraordinary knowledge of ornamental design which they display.

Many works have recently exhibited the Architectural wonders of those ages that have been misnamed "dark":—the profuse sculpture of the vast cathedrals—the massive grandeur of the feudal castles—the more recent magnificence of the Tudor and Elizabethan mansions, the châteaux of France, and palaces of Italy; but in all those delineations, the works of the earlier periods have been necessarily stripped of the charm of colour,—their salient feature,—as well as their painting, gilding, tapestry,—of all, in short, which imparted to them the finishing touch of splendour, and the peculiar impress of art in each successive phase of its progress; for those elaborate and beautiful efforts of artistic skill of the early portion of the middle ages have nearly all perished by barbarism or puritanical fanaticism, even where time had spared them. And yet, monuments of those branches of early art are not entirely lost to us; for examples of the style and taste of each period are vividly preserved in the splendid Illuminated MSS. of each succeeding era, which, in fact, contain the only records of the early history of modern painting, and yet lie buried in the great libraries of Europe, utterly inaccessible to thousands fully capable of appreciating their interest and beauty.

A selection from the most wonderful and splendid of these elaborate monuments of art—many of which have cost the entire life of a consummate artist to produce—will form the subject of the present work. No illustrated and general Historical Account of Illuminated MSS. has hitherto been attempted in this country; and, in France, the great works of BASTARD and SILVESTRE have but exhibited fragments, which, although each beautifully executed individually, are so placed together that they do not convey, except in a very few instances, the slightest idea of the artistic arrangement of a page of the MS. from which they are taken, whilst the immense price of these works confines them to a few great libraries. It may be fairly stated, therefore, that no work in any country has attempted to illustrate the subject with so large a number of magnificent specimens—each of the size of the originals;—each exhibiting the Miniature Pictures, graceful Borderings, and Illuminated Capitals of an entire, unmutilated Page, and, at the same time, at a price that will place the work within the reach of every Family Library. The Illustrations will form a splendid Series of Examples of the pictorial and decorative skill of the principal nations

Illuminated Books published by Messrs. Longman and Co.

of Europe (with some Eastern examples) from that period when the energetic nations of the North caught up and rekindled the expiring sparks of Roman art into successive phases of original and various beauty, to the commencement of the seventeenth century, when the progress of the newly invented art of Printing, and other causes, combined to put an end to the production of these extraordinary books: from which period, in short, *original art gradually declined.*

In addition to the illustration of the Progress of Art, which will be thus splendidly exhibited, the Plates will necessarily possess a great Historical interest. Associated as many of these gorgeous books are with the names and deeds of a host of the well-known heroes of Chivalry and Romance, our examples will of necessity form a sort of glittering pictorial history of the Dresses, Manners, and Customs of Europe, throughout the Middle Ages; frequently exhibiting authentic Portraits of historical personages of this and other European countries, of which no other such record remains: in so much that many will find in this work a Portrait Gallery of their illustrious ancestors, whose deeds, connected with the story of the land, or the great events of European or Asiatic warfare, are recorded in the superbly Illuminated Chronicles from which many of our subjects will be selected. But, above all, this selection will be deeply interesting on account of the noble specimens it will exhibit of the most celebrated and beautifully Illuminated MSS. of the BIBLE, from the time of St. Jerome to the end of the Sixteenth Century—wonderful monuments of the extraordinary labour and often exquisite skill which our earnest forefathers so profusely bestowed upon the embellishment of the Sacred volume.

Conditions of Publication.

The work will be issued in Parts, at intervals of about two months, each Part to cont in Three Plates, of the exact size of the original subjects, and each Plate accompanied by a description, with some account of the MS. from which it is taken. The work to be completed in Twenty-four Parts; the first to contain an Historical Sketch of the Progress of the Art of Illumination, with a Table illustrating the Plates in Chronological Order, as, in the Parts themselves, for the sake of variety and convenience, be issued without regard to their Chronological arrangement.

Each Part, containing Three Plates, with Descriptions, Imperial Quarto, (15 in. by 11), splendidly printed, in gold, silver, and colours, in imitation of the originals, as accurate as can be produced by art. Seventy guineas. 1s.

LARGE PAPER, on Half Imperial colombo, 1s. 6d., to prevent folding the large Plates, 2s.

Every Six Parts will form a truly gorgeous volume; four such Volumes completing the work.

Twenty-four Parts are thus proposed as the extent of the work, the smallest space in which justice can be done to the subject; but should the work not meet with the encouragement which is confidently expected, the Publishers reserve to themselves the privilege of completing it in a smaller compass.

PLATES CONTAINED IN THE FIRST PART.

1. Page from a large and beautiful MS. executed for Edward IV., containing Portraits of himself, and his brothers Gloucester and Clarence.
2. Page from a rich MS. of the Orations of Demosthenes, made for one of the Farnesi.
3. A remarkable Frontispiece, of great beauty, from a Venetian Diploma.

*** No. 2. containing a page from the fine copy of "Les Merveilles du Monde," presented by Jean sans Peur to his uncle the Duke of Berri, now preserved in the Royal Library of Paris, and some fine and interesting specimens from MSS. in British collections, will be ready in *December.*

"We have seen some specimens of a proposed work by Mr. Humphreys, on Illuminated MSS., which have surprised us by the accuracy of their execution, and the effect obtained by merely mechanical means."—*Quarterly Review*, June 1844.

II.
THE SERMON ON THE MOUNT.
[ST. MATTHEW, Chaps. v. vi. vii.]

Intended as a Birth-day Present or Gift-Book for all Seasons.

PRINTED IN GOLD AND COLOURS, IN THE MISSAL STYLE, WITH ORNAMENTAL BORDERS BY
OWEN JONES, ARCHITECT,

And a DESIGN from a Drawing by W. BOXALL, Esq.

Small 8vo. 21s. bound in an appropriate manner by Hayday; or 14s. in boards.

III.
REYNARD THE FOX:
A renowned Apologue of the early Middle Ages,

Reproduced in Rhyme, chiefly from the Low German Original of H. von ALKMAR. Embellished throughout with
ILLUMINATED WOOD-BLOCK LETTERS OF THE TWELFTH AND THIRTEENTH CENTURIES:
WITH AN INTRODUCTION.

By SAMUEL NAYLOR, late of Queen's College, Oxford.

Small 4to. pp. 360. elegantly bound in stamped vellum cloth.

LONDON: LONGMAN, BROWN, GREEN, AND LONGMANS.

Watson and Ogilvie, 97, Skinner Street, London.

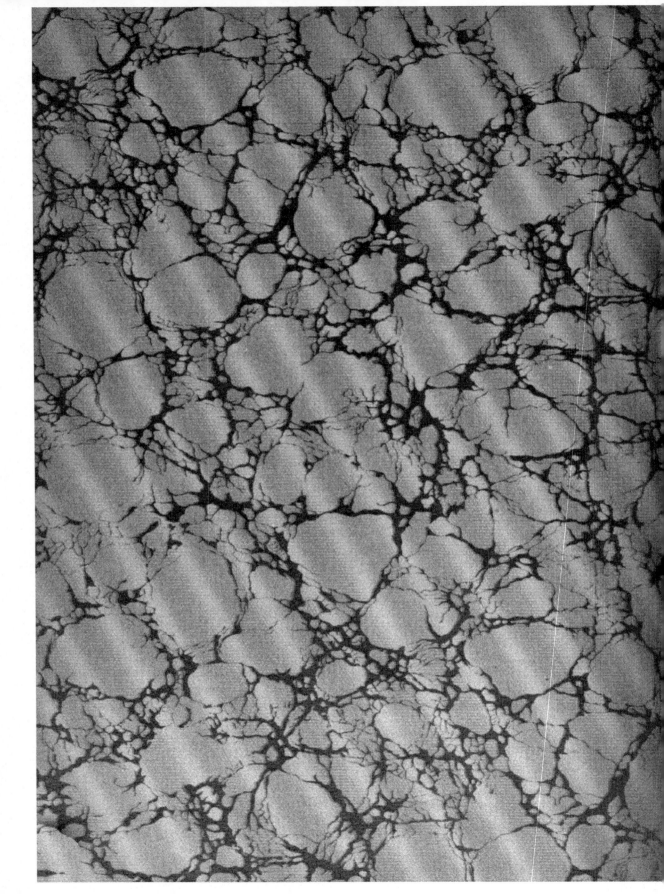

Lightning Source UK Ltd.
Milton Keynes UK
UKOW04f1931280417

300156UK00007B/151/P